Baby Animals

By Richard Roe

Random House New York

Library of Congress Cataloging in Publication Data: Roe, Richard, 1959– . Baby animals. SUMMARY: A collection of drawings of animal mothers and their babies. 1. Animals—Infancy—Pictorial works—Juvenile literature. [1. Animals—Infancy—Pictorial works] I. Title. QL763.R63   1985   599′.0334   85-2223   ISBN: 0-394-86956-7 (trade); 0-394-96956-1 (lib. bdg.)
Manufactured in the United States of America   1 2 3 4 5 6 7 8 9 0

Baby rabbits are called bunnies.
When they're very young, they stay
close to their mother.

Piglets have lots of brothers and sisters!

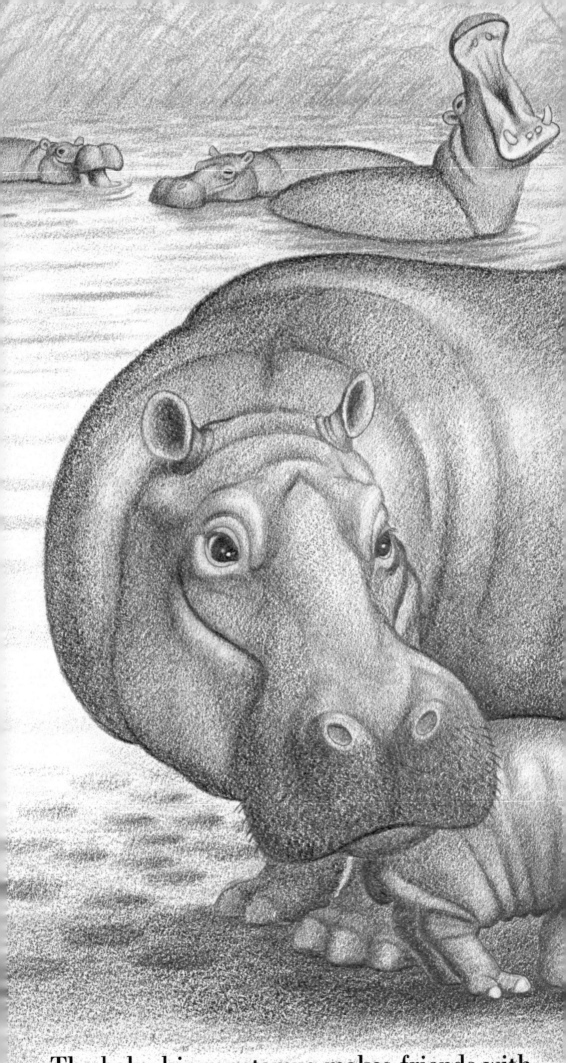

The baby hippopotamus makes friends with a mother goose and her four goslings.

Baby foxes are called kits.
They love to play with each other.

The chimpanzee mother teaches her
young chimp to swing.

Koala bears live in Australia. They carry
their young on their backs.

These three baby skunks have never seen
a grasshopper before.

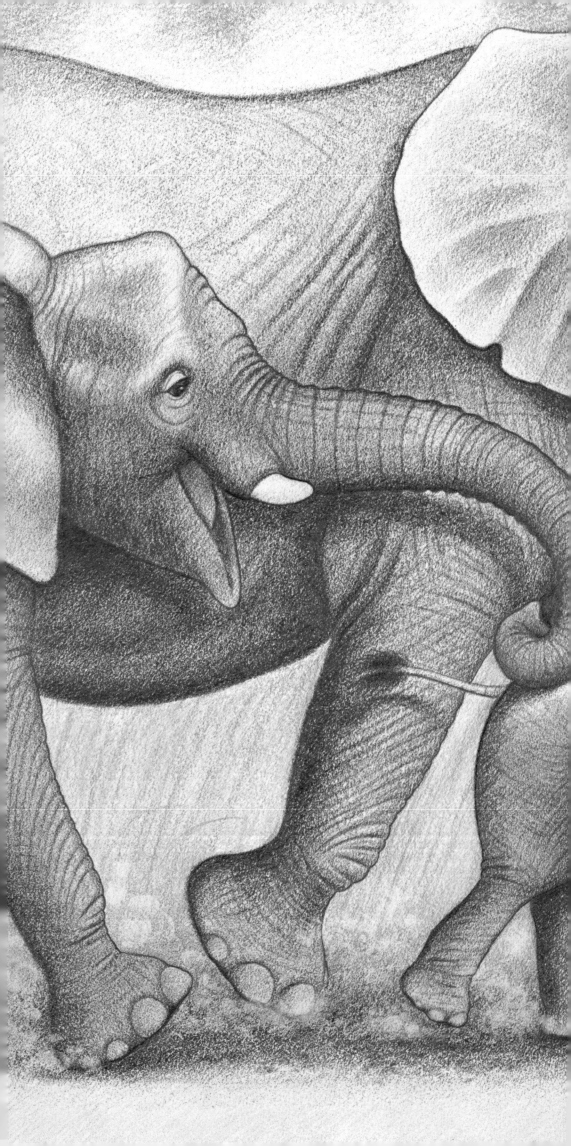

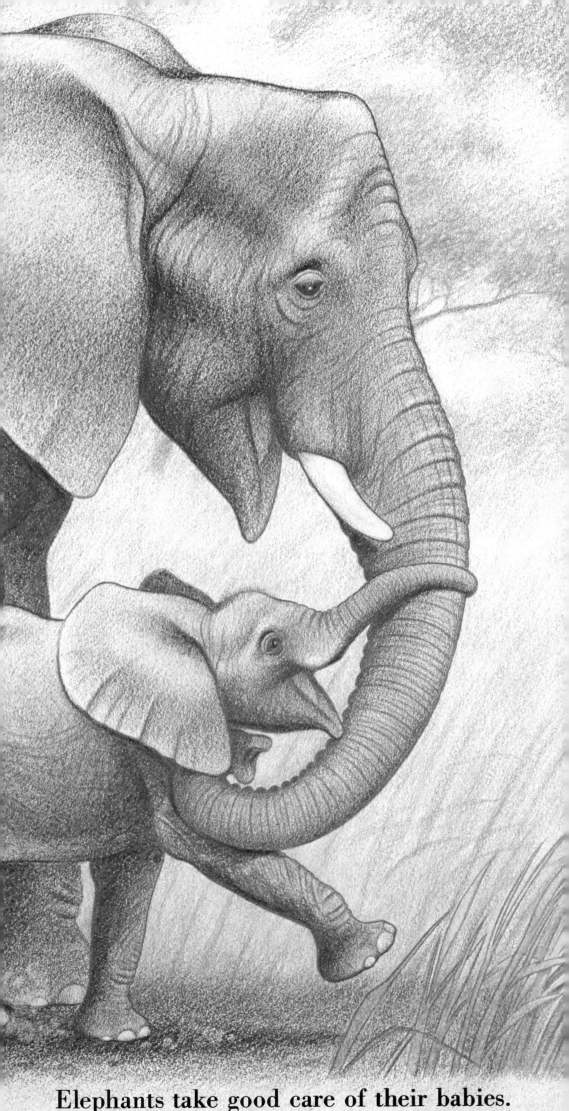

Elephants take good care of their babies.

Penguins live at the South Pole, where it is very cold. The baby penguin huddles under its mother to keep warm.

Polar bears live at the North Pole. This baby
polar bear likes to stay close to its mother.

The mother leopard is very tired, but her
two cubs want to play with her.

Did you know that
raccoons like to climb trees?